CONTENT

INTRODUCTION

Fairy tales have been a part of my life for as long as I can remember. I still reminisce about sitting in a room with cork lined walls that smelled like a forest and having a family friend read me tales by the Brothers Grimm and Hans Christian Andersen. Even at a young age I was always attracted to the dark ones—the stories where there was blood and pain and villains got what they deserved. I wanted iron shoes and nail studded barrels.

As an adult I discovered the award winning dark reimaginings of fairy tales in the anthology collections edited by Terri Windling and Ellen Datlow. They were filled with stories from long ago, but somehow made contemporary. These were the stories I wanted to write. I read Angela Carter's *The Bloody Chamber* and I wanted to *be* her. My mother has always maintained that my stories were "creepy." I take that as a compliment.

This anthology of tales came about over several years. Some were inspired by events from my life or the lives of female friends, others were ripped from contemporary headlines. I looked at the fact that in 2019 there is still a significant pay gap between women and men, especially in top level professions. I watched as the country of my birth became more and more like a dystopian tale by Margaret Atwood as women's bodies became less and less their own. I got sad, I got angry and then I picked up my pen.

We are all wounded in one way or another. I wanted these tales to open those wounds and examine them and see how much things have changed and then look at how far we still have to go.

Thank you for coming on this journey with me.

Heather

It Felt Like a Kiss

Out of all the princesses in the land, he chose me. He'd spent years looking for the right one. A real princess. I was minor royalty from a tiny impoverished kingdom in the far north. A nobody. Forgettable. I was nothing special until he hit me.

I remember our first date so clearly. He took me to Paris to Chez Pierre. Paris! I had never been out of the country before. We flew on his private jet. It was all so new to me. My grandmother dug her nails into my wrist before I left and hissed that I must make a good impression. This might be my only chance for happiness. Her grip had left a bracelet of purple bruises around my wrist. At the table he tenderly took my hand and caressed each bruise with a kiss.

"So beautiful..." he murmured as he squeezed until the bone snapped. This is how he knew I was the one. The others, they bruised. But I broke. I was a delicate flower. I was perfect.

Fighting back tears, he took me in his arms and proposed right away. My wrist began to swell, and we left the restaurant and flew to the finest hospital in the land. You should have seen how gentle he was. How softly he held me. How tenderly he caressed my body as I waited for the bone to be set in plaster. The tears were spilling from his eyes like water.

"So beautiful..."

In my grandmother's day they made you sleep on a bed with twenty mattresses and a tiny dried pea underneath. You were supposed to feel the pea as if it were a boulder and wake up black and blue. It was a charade. No one, not even a real princess, can feel a pea under twenty mattresses. Girls in those days helped each other.

"Servant girls would come into your room after dark and beat you, but only if they liked you," my grandmother cackled. "That's why you should always be kind to the help. Make a good impression on them and they will serve you faithfully." She recalled her own courtship with my grandfather as I was being prepared for my date with the prince.

"I made sure to ingratiate myself to the girl who was assigned to me as lady's maid. As soon as she unpacked my travelling bag—which only contained enough for a one night stay—I presented her with a necklace. The trinket was cheap but pretty." She began to vigorously comb my titian hair and wind it up into an elaborate tower. "That night she came to me—Elsa I think her name was—with a stone that she'd pulled from the garden wall. We put a leather strap between my teeth to stop me crying out and she beat me with the stone until I was pebbled with bruises." She stopped to adjust the pins and admire her handiwork. "The next morning, I said I'd slept badly. I had the bruises to prove it, so your grandfather proposed."

"Did they know? I mean, did they realise it was a deception?"

My grandmother snorted. "Of course they knew. Every woman who had ever married into royalty knew. That's how they snagged their prince. Deception. But the men? I don't think they ever did."

"Did you have to keep bruising yourself?"

She placed a strand of pearls, our only family heirloom, around my neck. "No, back then once was enough. You just had to prove you were a real princess. It's not like today." She cast a glance towards my mother who removed the ice pack from her blackened eye and nodded solemnly.

On our wedding day he placed his hands around my throat and squeezed until I could not draw breath. He let go, and I gasped as he sighed.

"Your neck is like a swan. So beautiful..." he whispered into my ear. His fingerprints blossomed at my tender throat. How I loved him.

Once a year I am permitted to travel north and visit my mother. She is a shadow. She lurks in corners and cringes. She wears her bruises with shame. How can she not see how much my father loves her?

When I get home my prince will be waiting. He has missed me so much. His delicate flower has come home to him at last. I will wear white because I know it pleases him. He loves the look of scarlet blood on snow white cloth. He will strike me—one blow for every day that we were apart —and then with all the tenderness there is, take me in his arms.

Life's Rich Pageant

Time had tried
To etch his name
Across her face,
But found it
Too flat
Too smooth
A Botoxed canvas.

She was fading.
Her mirror told her so.
Repeatedly.
Motherhood
(or rather Step Motherhood)
Was taking its toll.
No amount of spray tan
Could stop the inevitable decline.

She'd married the girl's father
When she was eighteen.
Fresh from the Pageant scene.
But now she was
Thirty-three
And fading rapidly.
She saw how he looked
At his own offspring and she thought
He'd soon be trading her in for a
younger model.

The girl was radiant
Like the sun and
She planned to burn her light out
The only way she knew how:
Beauty Pageants.

The child, now sixteen,
Sun kissed and haloed by a mane
Of golden curls was given
A makeover.

Her flaxen hair was dyed
Black as a raven's wing.
The blacker the dye, the
Higher the chance of

Contracting bladder cancer.
I hope it's painful.
She thought.

A perfectly manicured hand
Powdered the young face
Milk white
(it rarely snows in Texas,
But cows are big business)
And gashed her lips red
With Chanel.
She'd read
That red lipstick
Contained lead.
I hope she chokes on it, she said.

The child was put on a strict diet
Of celery
And water.
She refused to vomit
Despite being shown how to,
So the Stepmother had to resort to
Laxatives.

Her healthy frame
Withered away.
She was a bag of bones
As black as ebony
As white as the moon
As red as blood.
(Except there was no monthly blood.
Her weight loss saw to that.)

When at last
She was "perfect"
Perfectly repulsive
The Step-Monster thought,
She was entered in a
Universal Royalty pageant.

Now, who's the fairest
Of them all, she croaked
To herself through a haze of
Cigarettes and
Diet coke.

You can imagine
Her surprise
When her stepdaughter
Was awarded the

Top prize
Of an artificial rhinestone tiara,
A satin monogrammed banner
And a modelling contract
From Prince Charming and Associates.
(She couldn't show her astonishment
because
Her face didn't move above the eyebrows.)

They loved her gothic,
Skeletal frame
And bruised eyes
Like she'd cried all night.

It was rumoured that her faded
Stepmother had once been Miss Texas,
But she was a pile of garbage
Compared to the sullen, bitter flower
that lay before them.

And lay before them she would.
Every man in the office
Would have a piece of her
Before her modelling contract was up.
The camera loved the damaged look,
All red eyed and furious.

Her self-harming scars becoming the
Newest fashion accessory
For the Tween set.

And the Stepmother?
Her husband left her
The next year
For a girl half her age
Who looked just like his daughter.
She died in '95
From a liposuction gone awry.
Her stepdaughter later committed suicide.

Happily ever after is a lie.

The Trial of Emily Scarlett, part 1

Bailiff: All rise. Superior Court of the state of North Carolina is now in session, the honourable Judge Hunter presiding. Please be seated.

Judge: What have we got on tap for today, then?

Bailiff: Your Honour, today's case is People v Kurt Wolfson.

Judge: Ah, yes. The quarterback. Mr Wolfson, how do you plead to the charges against you?

Kurt Wolfson: Not guilty, Your Honour.

Judge: Proceed with opening remarks.

District Attorney: Your Honour and ladies and gentlemen of the jury: the defendant has been charged with the crime of rape. This is a particularly heinous crime because the victim was unconscious at the time that the act took place. The evidence I present will prove to you that the defendant is guilty as charged.

Defence Counsel: Your Honour and members of the jury: under the law my client is presumed innocent until proven guilty. During this trial, you will hear no real evidence against my client. He and the woman in question had consensual sex after they both had been drinking heavily at a graduation party. In fact, I will prove that my client is the real victim here because her accusations have left his reputation in tatters. My client is not guilty of rape.

Judge: Call your first witness.

District Attorney: The people call Emily Scarlett.

Clerk: Please stand. Raise your right hand. Do you promise that the testimony you shall give in the case before this court shall be the truth, the whole truth, and nothing but the truth, so help you God?

Emily Scarlett: I do.

Clerk: Please state your full name.

Emily Scarlett: Emily Ann Scarlett.

Clerk: You may be seated.

District Attorney: Can you tell me in your own words what happened the night of May 27th, 2017?

Emily Scarlett: It was a Saturday. Graduation had been the night before and Stubby was having a party out in woods to celebrate.

District Attorney: And by Stubby you mean Charles Stubbins, isn't that correct?

Emily Scarlett: Yes, sorry. Charles Stubbins. We call him Stubby. His family owns a little cabin out in woods. His grandmother used to live there before she died last year. Ever since then Stubby uses it as a place to party.

District Attorney: You had been there before?

Emily Scarlett: Yes. Many times.

District Attorney: What happened on the night in question?

Emily Scarlett: Stubby and Perky...I mean Lionel Perkins...built a bonfire in the woods outside the cabin. They filled the house with alcohol and invited the whole senior class out for one last bash before we all went our separate ways.

District Attorney: Go on.

Emily Scarlett: I got there about seven o'clock. Lots of people had been there all afternoon. I just wanted to relax after all the stress of finals.

District Attorney: Were you drinking?

Emily Scarlett: Yes. This time I was. I don't normally drink when we go out partying. I usually am the designated driver, but my friend Cindy Ellison drove this time, so I decided to let my hair down. I didn't mean to get to so drunk.

District Attorney: Go on.

Emily Scarlett: I thought there would be food at the cabin, but there wasn't. Just

19

alcohol. I guess I'm kind of lightweight because I had a couple drinks on an empty stomach, and I was feeling really out of it.

District Attorney: Do you remember meeting the accused?

Emily Scarlett: Yes. Early in the evening. He came over to me and Cindy and tried to hit on us. He was saying it was our last chance to...am I allowed to say what he said? It's really rude.

District Attorney: Please say exactly what he said to you.

Emily Scarlett: He said it was our last chance to "fuck the quarterback."

District Attorney: Go on.

Emily Scarlett: We just blew him off. Everyone knows what those football players are like. They screw as many girls as they can and then laugh about it with all their friends.

Defence Counsel: Objection! Hearsay.

Judge: Sustained. Please stick to the facts.

District Attorney: Can you tell us what happened later in the evening?

Emily Scarlett: It's not really clear. I kept drinking. I had some beers followed by a bottle of Boone's Farm. I think it was Strawberry Hill. Anyway, I remember that I wanted to find Cindy but didn't know where she was. I was feeling sick. I might have vomited. I'm not sure. I decided to wander away from the bonfire and back towards the car. It was so hot. The music was loud, and my head was pounding. That's all I can remember.

District Attorney: What is the next thing you remember?

Emily Scarlett: I was on a gurney in a hallway. A nurse was cleaning the grazes on my knees. There was a bandage on my head. I thought I'd been hurt. Like in a car accident or something. I just kept asking for Cindy to make sure she was okay. The nurse told me I had been assaulted. I just couldn't believe it.

District Attorney: Go on.

Emily Scarlett: I wanted to go to the bathroom, but they wouldn't let me. They said they had to collect evidence first. I had bruises on my thighs and my knee was cut really bad. They needed pictures. (murmurs indistinctly)

District Attorney: I'm sorry, Miss Scarlett. I need to ask you to speak up, please.

Emily Scarlett: (clears throat) I said they had to swab me down below for semen. It was...humiliating because I hadn't ever let anyone touch me down there before. They had to give me morphine just to do the swabs because I wouldn't stop screaming from the pain. I overheard one of the nurses say that when the ambulance brought me in there had been a stick the size of her arm inside me. (winces)

Defence Counsel: Objection! Hearsay!

Judge: Sustained. I won't warn you again, young lady.

District Attorney: Go on, Miss Scarlett.

Emily Scarlett: When they finally let me go to the restroom it hurt to pee. To urinate. It burned. They made me do a pregnancy test and then had me tested for HIV as they said they didn't know what all I had been penetrated with. I stopped to look at myself in the mirror and there were pine needles in my hair. I just kept thinking they must have fallen from a tree. We were in the woods. How else could they have gotten there? I just couldn't believe it had happened. (starts to cry)

District Attorney: Do you need a moment, Miss Scarlett?

Emily Scarlett: No. I can continue.

District Attorney: Take your time.

Emily Scarlett: That's really it. I was given some hospital scrubs to wear because they needed to keep my clothes as evidence. I signed a police report and was sent home. I didn't find out about who it was that had raped me until I saw it on the news. I had no idea that Charles and Lionel had caught him and pulled him off me and called 911.

District Attorney: Thank you Miss Scarlett. Your witness.

Defence Counsel: Emily, how old are you?

Emily Scarlett: I'm eighteen years old.

Defence Counsel: And what is your occupation?

Emily Scarlett: I guess I'm a student. I graduated from Forest Hills High School in May of last year and I'm a freshman at Wake Forest University. I'm going to be a kindergarten teacher.

Defence Counsel: So, this supposed "rape" hasn't affected your ability to go off to college?

Emily Scarlett: No...I mean...yes.

Defence Counsel: Answer the question, Miss Scarlett. Is it yes or is it no?

District Attorney: I object Your Honour. He's badgering the witness.

Judge: Overruled. The witness will answer.

Emily Scarlett: Um, well no. I mean...I am still going to Wake Forest. But yes...it has affected—

Defence Counsel: So, you can still go on to university, unlike my client who had his scholarship revoked due to the negative publicity surrounding his arrest.

District Attorney: I renew my objection, Your Honour.

Judge: Noted. Please continue.

Defence Counsel: I'll change tack, Your Honour. You said in your testimony that you had been drinking. That you were drunk. Is that true?

Emily Scarlett: Um...yes, but—

Defence Counsel: What were you wearing the night of the alleged assault?

Emily Scarlett: What was I wearing? Um...a red dress.

Defence Counsel: A red mini-dress, I believe.

Emily Scarlett: Yes. It was a mini-dress. But—

Defence Counsel: Quite a short mini-dress. Exhibit A, Your Honour.

Judge: Thank you.

Defence Counsel: What else were you wearing? I presume you wore something underneath.

District Attorney: Objection! Relevance.

Judge: Overruled. The dress is quite short. It goes to character. The witness will answer.

Emily Scarlett: As well as the dress I was wearing underwear, a bra and a pair of gold ballerina flats. Oh, and a thin cardigan. It can get chilly at night in the woods.

Defence Counsel: And were they sexy underwear?

District Attorney: Objection!

Judge: Overruled. Goes to character. A short skirt can lead a man on. The witness will answer.

Emily Scarlett: I don't know. I don't think so. They were black. They weren't lacy or anything. Just black.

Defence Counsel: And where were these 'black but not lacy' underwear when you were brought to the hospital?

Emily Scarlett: (murmurs indistinctly)

Defence Counsel: Speak up, please Miss Scarlett.

Emily Scarlett: I don't know.

Defence Counsel: You don't know? You don't know where your underwear were?

Emily Scarlett: I wasn't wearing them when I was brought to hospital.

Defence Counsel: You weren't wearing them? So, you had willingly taken them off earlier in the evening.

Emily Scarlett: No! I mean...I don't know. I don't remember. He must have taken them off me!

Defence Counsel: Now Miss Scarlett, how can that be? You said it yourself. You don't remember.

Emily Scarlett: He must have done. I wouldn't have. I'm not like that.

Defence Counsel: Well, what are you like? I mean a young girl, in a tight red mini-dress with sexy black underwear looking for a good time at the last party of the year before you go off to college. A girl who drinks to the point of blacking out. There is no telling what sort of girl you are.

District Attorney: Objection!

Defence Counsel: Withdrawn. Were the clothes you were wearing that night returned to you after your stay in hospital?

Emily Scarlett: Not my dress. It was kept for evidence. But my shoes and bra and cardigan were.

Defence Counsel: But not your underwear?

Emily Scarlett: No.

Defence Counsel: The police searched the woods, but your underwear were never found. Is that correct?

Emily Scarlett: No.

Defence Counsel: No, they didn't search the woods, Miss Scarlett?

Emily Scarlett: No...I mean yes they did search the woods, but no they never found them.

Defence Counsel: I put it to you that they were never found because you were not wearing any that night. I put it to you Miss Scarlett that you went to that graduation party planning to have sex with my client or someone like him. I put it to you that you got exactly what you wanted. You bedded the quarterback. You're practically famous.

District Attorney: Objection! Your Honour, he is badgering the witness.

Emily Scarlett: (sobs)

Defence Counsel: No further question.

The State You're In

Young girl
You gaze out at the world
With coal black eyes
That burn with
Hatred and fear,
The cause of all your
Nightmares and tears.
He is no father of yours.

Your mother
Let go of your hand
And departed this small-minded life
For more green and pleasant lands.
He said he was lonely.
You were dutiful.
Up to a point.
But then.
But then.
But then.

At church
All the men say
What a good daughter you are
To look after your father
So well.
What a fine wife you will make
Some day.
If only they knew.
Maybe they do.

Two months pass by
As clear as the sky.
You check down below for
The tell-tale stripe,
But there is no sign.
No blood to be found.

What do you do?
You have to know,
You shoplift a test (the only way)
As every store in
This one-horse town has
A deacon,
A busy-body,
Or a friend of your father.
Word gets around.

Late,
After dark,
When he has come and gone
From this unholy marital bed
You piss on a stick
And wait.
Two lines confirm
What you already knew.
Do you stay
And pray
That this demon seed
Inside of you
Will go away?
Or do you run?

Young girl
With the coal black eyes
Burn your bridges.
Wear your disguise.
A donkey skin,
The hide of a deer,
The pelts of a thousand animals
Slain by your father deep in the woods,

The clothes of your mother
Which make you appear
Older than your sixteen years.
Swallow your fears
And leave the State
You're in.

Perchance to Dream

I have always suffered from melancholy, just like my mother. She was a solemn child with moist glassy eyes, but her tears never fell until she met my father. At the age of sixteen, the age I am now, she was taken from her home and wed to a man thrice her age. A man who had no time for feminine weakness, no understanding of tears. He was fond of the phrase "pull yourself together," and used it often which only brought more tears from my mother. How could he not understand the dark clouds that filled her head with fear and sadness?

After two years of marriage she would not rise from the bed and spent her days weeping silently into her pillow. She said her heart was beating like a captive bird and if she got up and sat in a chair the bird would crack open the cage of her ribs and fly out of her chest. She must lie still at all costs or else she would surely die. My father's solution was to make her with child. He reasoned she was suffering from ennui and would "snap out of it" (another of his pet phrases) if she had a baby to care for. He spilled his seed into her at every opportunity while tears squeezed from the corners of her red-rimmed eyes into her ebony hair and her fingernails pressed into her palms until she drew blood.

Eventually she did get out of the bed, but only because the pain was too great to lie down with her expanding belly that stretched her skin as tightly as it stretched her fears. My father was triumphant. He was so pleased to see her sewing by the window in the cool autumn air that he left her alone. He never saw the trembling of her pale hands and the tangle of her jet-black hair or the way she spent hours pricking her finger over and over and watching the blood drip onto the window ledge. She could feel me stirring inside her and she was afraid that I was covered with the darkness that filled her body like smoke from a coal fire.

In the bleak midwinter, she was seen to open the window and stare out at the blanket of snow for hours as I lay at her feet in my wooden cradle. She would be found in nothing but her shift, her skin like an opal and the tears frozen on her face. My cradle would be covered in snow, but I never cried out. I just stared up at my father with solemn, unblinking eyes that were moist and glassy with tears that never fell. Years later, when he made a remark about the happiest years of her life, she slowly turned and spoke to him. It was the first time she had spoken directly to him since their marriage had begun. He thought all this feminine nonsense of tears and birds in rib cages was past. She laughed, tossing back her ebony hair to show the pearl of her throat and then dived out of the open window into the frozen snow with her blood spilling out of her like wine.

I was a solemn child and now a solitary one after my mother's brave leap. My father could no longer bear to look upon my face and he spat upon the ground at the mention of her name. He said the devil had bewitched my mother and he believed I was cursed as well. I awoke every day with a face washed by the sea. My father growled like a beast when he saw my shining face in the mornings. She too had drowned herself in saltwater. It is a wonder the tide did not take her sooner. At the age of twelve, I began to sleep with the pillow over my face in the hopes that I would suffocate in the night and then be able to sleep forever. My father soon put a stop to that when he brought home Priscilla.

Priscilla had been an old school-friend of my mother. She was to be my governess so that he did not have to look after me. My father hoped that Priscilla would bring joy back to me, but it nearly drove me into madness. The more she was soft with kindness, the harder like flint I became inside. She would bring me sweetmeats to tempt me to eat, but it was all poison in my mouth. A thunderstorm raged within my skull and beat me with the words of *Die! Die! Useless girl! Worthless creature!* and I found the only way to scatter the clouds was to work. I began to clean the hearth and scrubbed until my knuckles bled.

Every night Priscilla would call out, "Poor child, can you find no rest?" and I would cry in her lap until golden slumber overtook me. I found that if I poured all the lentils and beans into the ashes, I could spend all day plucking them out. I picked at pulses until my fingers were as crooked as a twig and I was covered in ash. My tears traced a river down my sooty face as I laboured. She carried me to the bath and bathed me like I was a new-born babe, but still I grew darker and darker within. As she bathed me, she would say, "Poor child, leave that job for the birds." But alas, I could not. Only if I worked myself into a frenzy would the clouds recede and show a glimmer of light. At my father's orders all hearth tools were taken away, so I cleaned the stone floors with my bare palms until they shredded like cheese. I cleaned the ash with my tongue. I lay down in the dust to die and Priscilla saved my life.

When I was fourteen, she took me out to the woods and left me. Not to die, but to live. To be away from the oppressive memory of my mother's death and a father who hated the sight of me. She took me to a little cottage and left me there. She then killed a hare with her bare hands and told my father that I had run away into the woods and been killed by a beast. She showed the hare's heart and murmured sadly, "It is so stunted because her heart was broken," and he believed her.

When the wee men came home, I was sitting in the ashes and scratching my arm with a sharp stone. They said nothing and ate cold supper that night. Being away from the ghost of my mother parted the shadows and I awoke less afraid. When I opened my eyes, they were crowded round my bed, and one took my arm and began to clean it so lovingly with a damp cloth soaked in healing herbs that it felt like a doe licking her fawn. Their kindness was a balm to my soul.

The first few days I did nothing except sit in the ashes, but when they came home from their long day in the mines they were as black as I was, and we had a little laugh. A laugh! I had forgotten that I could laugh. After many weeks I was able to get up and work inside the little cottage. At first, I was afraid to touch the broom for fear that the frenzy would come over me, but soon I found I could work and rest and there was no feverish rage to enclose me. After many months, I was able to see the blue sky in the little window of my soul and I felt a peace that I had only known before in slumber. I cooked supper for the first time since I had arrived and when they returned, they looked upon me and smiled and one of them said in a voice so low it was like a whisper of the breeze in the leaves of a tree, "We know what it is like to feel pain," and we never spoke of it again.

After a year of living in the woods, Priscilla came to see me. I had been outside tending the garden and singing to myself. I was so changed she almost didn't recognise me. She was wearing my father's ring and I could see she was to be my mother now. Seeing her opened up a little bottle of oily black smoke that I did not even know was still within me.

Mechanically, I sat down and let her brush my hair and weave it with fine ribbons that she had brought. My heart began that old hammering and my skin grew cold and bloodless, but still she chatted gaily about life at the manor and what a gem my father was. How telling him I was dead was the best thing she could have done because look how kind it had made my father and look how happy I had become. She kissed me goodbye and went on her way never noticing that tendrils of ebony smoke were creeping around me like vines. I took the ribbons from my hair and tied them round my throat and waited for the hazy slumber of death to take me in.

I was found a few hours later, blue but still breathing when the men came home. Their eyes were full of sorrow, but they said nothing. Instead they removed all the knives and took the laces from my boots. From then on, I stayed in bed and wet my pillow with my tears just as my mother had before I was born. One of the men always stayed behind to watch over me. Food was again poison in my mouth and my arms were raw from scratching them. They could only shake their heads and wonder what had caused this relapse.

By the time the leaves were a blanket on the ground and a nip was in the air I was able to sit up in bed. My tears were dry, but my heart continued to be heavy. The men had all returned to the mines when my tears ceased to flow, but still they knew I was not completely well. Early one morning there was a sound like thunder and the door flew open to reveal my stepmother with a basket of apples from my mother's orchard. She breezed in, slid her finger along the mantlepiece and wrinkled her nose at the accumulation of dust. Was this the woman who had tenderly looked after me as if I were her own child? Had she ever cared for me or had she planned to be rid of me and have my mother's life all to herself? She gave me a crimson apple, as red as the blood that had flowed from my mother when she leapt into the arms of God and away from this life of sorrow and pain. I ate it, tasting my mother's blood in every bite. She departed as abruptly as she entered and said if I could not be more sociable then she would never return. I stared at the core in my hand and dug at a seed with my nail. I knew what I had to do. I put the apple core into my mouth and swallowed.

What followed was like a dream. I floated away into a land of milk and honey where everything was as bright as the sun. I saw my mother. Her face was golden like an angel, so different from the wild and frantic face awash with blood that haunted all my waking dreams. She spoke of peace. She spoke of joy. She said that in this golden slumber I would lose all the earthy shackles that had bound me. There was so much light here that there was no room for darkness. I do not know how long I lay in this blissful sleep of near death. I had many dreams that flowed through me like water.

I dreamt I was in a glass case and all the angels of Heaven came to me and gave me gifts that would help drive away the darkness. One gave me a ball of light to carry in my hand. Another gave me a glowing halo to wear upon my head. My mother kissed my forehead and I was filled with radiance like a candle in a gourd. God reached down and took me in His mighty hands and raised me from the glass enclosure and planted me in the earth. I was a tree and my feet took root while my body became the trunk. I could see myself in the forest reaching up with my branches to my mother in Heaven. Suddenly, the world was plunged into blackness. A lumberjack was chopping me with his axe. I could feel him splitting me up the middle and the sap oozing down my trunk. I lifted my head to cry out and the core dislodged from my throat. I tried to sit up, but my skirts had been pulled over my head. Then he stood up and spat on the ground. Clumsily, I sat up and stared at this man who looked so like my father with his shaggy, greying beard and unkempt hair. He growled then picked me up, threw me onto the back of his horse and rode me far away to his manor house. I could feel the sea welling up behind my eyes again and all the demons that lurk in darkness were pricking at my skin. He saw me, desired me and had me. When we arrived at his house, he made me his wife.

Here I sit, the same age that my mother was when she was forced to live chained to a beast. I sit by the open window and put my hand on my swollen belly and breathe in the cool autumn air. He leaves me alone if he thinks I am knitting. But I am not knitting, I am biding my time. When the winter comes and the snow is soft like a feather blanket, my mother will call to me and I will rise and follow. I will toss back my ebony hair, lift up my head to show the pearl of my throat and then fly out the window into the arms of my mother.

Perception Filter

I wake up.

I take a selfie.

I look in the mirror.

I swipe to my favourite filters.

I swipe oil from my T-Zone.

I'm perfect.   I'm a disaster.

I love my   I hate my

huge, expressive eyes

piggy, bloodshot eyes

fringed with thick lashes,

with invisible lashes,

button nose,

crooked nose,

full, sensuous red lips.

non-existent upper lip.

46

This is what I see.

A beauty mark,

A hideous mole,

wavy golden blond hair,

lank dishwater blond hair,

a crown of flowers.

a crown of thorns.

I look at myself.

I'm a gorgeous beauty.
I'm a repulsive beast.

This is who I am.

The Curse Has Come Upon Me Cried

Susi felt utterly dejected. She had waited all summer for it to begin and it never happened. Her mother said she was just a "late bloomer." She said to "just give it some time." But Susi *had* waited. She couldn't be the only one who hadn't started. The first day of school was approaching. She would simply die if she was the only girl in the freshman class who hadn't started yet.

Her own best friend Gayl had gotten "the curse" right at the end of the eighth grade. If only Gayl hadn't started before her, they could have toughed it out together as freshman. But now, Gayl would be in another league altogether. She would be a woman. All the boys would make howling noises as she strutted past. Oh, it was too unbearable to contemplate!

The first day of school wasn't as bad as she had imagined. She was not the only one who had not begun to change. There were at least a dozen girls who looked like Susi—pale, thin girls with flat, angular bodies. Girls in jeans and ballet flats. Girls with their hair scraped back into a high ponytail. She felt conspicuous and invisible at the same time.

Physical education was the worst. The coaches made no allowance for non-developed bodies. All the activities were geared toward the more mature girls. They, with their strength and endurance, completed the tasks with ease while Susi was left panting and sweating. The changing room after lessons was an exercise in humiliation. The older girls with their rippling muscles and well- built bodies made Susi's ghostly, frail frame look like a scarecrow. She covered her hairless parts in shame.

These mature girls wielded a power that Susi simply did not possess. She watched them from the shadows as they stalked their prey— the boys. She admired their confidence; the way they walked, swishing their tails in a provocative way as the boys wolf-whistled at them. She had even seen Gayl turn a few heads. She felt that if she did not grow up soon, she would die.

On the third Tuesday in February, Susi awoke to a dull, heavy pain in her belly. It was a sensation she had never had before. She dressed and went to school, but by the end of her fourth period Biology class she had developed a pinching pain in her lower back. At lunch, she scanned the cafeteria for Gayl.

Gayl was tearing into her hamburger at a table surrounded by the popular crowd. Susi approached the table and Chennaya snarled, giving her a sideways look that told her she didn't belong, but she didn't care. She had to speak to Gayl. There was no one else she could ask. She described her symptoms as Gayl wolfed down her burger and fries. She replied with her mouth full. "Yup. It does sound like you're about to get cursed. Welcome to the club."

Susi gnawed at her cuticle thoughtfully.

"You'll have to stop that, you know."

Susi let her finger dangle at the corner of her mouth.

"Your nails. They'll grow harder, now. Duh!" Gayl replied as she wiggled a perfect set of ten dagger-like claws in Susi's bewildered face.

The pain in Susi's lower back was reaching an uncomfortable state. She held her belly and stumbled off to the toilets. As she glanced down in her panties, she saw a rusty brown stripe. *This is really it,* she thought to herself. *The curse has come upon me.* She felt relieved and frightened all at once.

Over the next few months, rapid changes began to happen to Susi's body. Hair grew in unexpected places. Her body filled out, it lengthened and strengthened in ways she had only dreamed of. Gayl had been right. Her nails grew long and sharp. Boys began to notice her. Dolph and Boris wolf-whistled at her outside the mall. Her hair grew longer and shaggier. Her jaw elongated to accommodate the ten extra teeth that she would need. Her bones grew too, reforming into a more lupine shape.

By June, she was a fully-fledged lycanthrope. She moved with the most popular pack and quickly secured her place as the alpha female. Kurt, the best-looking boy in school, admired her new physique and had grabbed her tail in a frisky way. That evening, under the full moon, she made him howl. She was no man's meat. She was powerful and fierce. She could run and fight as well as any man. She was Lupa the wolf goddess. She was finally a woman.

Author's note: *All the names used in the story are the words for wolf in other languages. Susi (Finnish), Gayl (Armenian), Chennaya (Malayalam), Dolph (Swedish), Boris (Bulgarian), and Kurt (Turkish) according to wolfsongalaska.org.*

Towering

As a Disciple of Truth
And a daughter of Eve,
I am fit for no purpose
Except wife and mother.

My price
(above rubies)
Lies between my legs
And my ability
To reproduce.
I am not to
Blink
    Think
        Shrink
From my appointed role.
This is what God made me for.

We grew up in a Tower
My sisters and I
Surrounded with high walls, gates and bars.
We lived in a bubble,
In our own measured world of
Black and white.
There was no grey. Just
Our right
     Their wrong
         Us
            Them

                Christian

                   Heathen.

Biblical in every word and deed.
The glory of our hair
An anaconda
That slithered down our backs.

At thirteen
A promise made.
A ring,
Pure silver
Like my virginity.

My father
    My guard
        My jailor
Jealously shielded my hymen
From interlopers.

My sisters and I
From our Ivory Tower
Dried our waterfall hair
Out of the narrow-minded window
And looked down at the passers-by
And sighed.

We were of this world but not in it.

At eighteen
I was courted by
A man of twenty-five.
We were not to
Talk
    Touch
        Tempt
One another.
Soon there was a wedding.
I was stamped
Property of my husband

As I traded one Tower for another.

My mother quivered
And told me that a Godly wife
Says YES to sex
Every
      Single
           Time
And so
After years of saying no
He is all over me
Like an insatiable rash.

I begin to bear
His heirs
And fulfil the role
That I was bred for.

He comes to me
Daily
      Nightly
           Roughly
                 Never Gently
And I open my legs
And my womb
To him.

I spend my days enclosed,
Wiping bottoms and noses
And tears.
(Mostly my own.)

He ventures forth
Into the daily world
A knight
In armour
That does not shine.

When he returns
I smell his whores upon his skin.
Their sweat
        Perfume
                And feral stink
As it mingles with my own.
He brings Babylon
Into our bed and
I endure.

What can I do?
Who can I tell?
The Pearls of Wisdom say

It is the wife to blame
When the husband strays.

At baby number four
A scandal breaks
My private shame
Now public.

I am disgraced and
He is whisked away
To get "help"
While I am left
Helpless
        Hopeless
                Alone.

I see the way they look at me.
Those Inside and Out both shake their
heads.
I wish I was dead.
Black and white.
There is no grey.
Those Outside say
"Why do you stay?"
And Inside just imply

"if you did more
He'd have no need of Godless whores."

The walls enclose.
I cannot breathe.
I cannot leave
The safety of this broken Tower.
What skills have I?
What can I do?
All I am is a fertile womb.

Divorce is a sin.

I am merely a Princess
Locked in a tower
Who will never be rescued.

What else can I do but jump?

The Trial of Emily Scarlett, part 2

Bailiff: All rise. Superior Court of the state of North Carolina is now in session, the honourable Judge Hunter presiding. Please be seated.

Judge: What's it to be today, then?

Bailiff: Your Honour, it's still People v Kurt Wolfson.

Judge: Ah, yes. The girl in the short red dress. Continue.

Defence Counsel: Your Honour, members of the jury, today we will look at my client and see that he is a young man who has had a grave wrong done to him. These slanderous remarks that he forced himself on Miss Emily Scarlett are outrageous. I will prove that she was a willing participant.

District Attorney: Your Honour and ladies and gentlemen of the jury, I will be proving that my client Miss Scarlett could not have consented as her blood alcohol level was so high that she was unconscious during their encounter.

Judge: Call your first witness.

Defence Counsel: The people call Kurt Wolfson.

Clerk: Please stand. Raise your right hand. Do you promise that the testimony you shall give in the case before this court shall be the truth, the whole truth, and nothing but the truth, so help you God?

Kurt Wolfson: I do.

Clerk: Please state your full name.

Kurt Wolfson: Kurt Stephen Wolfson.

Clerk: You may be seated.

Defence Counsel: Can you tell me in your own words what happened the night of May 27th, 2017?

Kurt Wolfson: Well, it was the night after graduation. Things were looking pretty sweet for me. I had been quarterback at Forest Hill High School, and I had a football scholarship to Duke. It was my last night to party with all my friends before we went our separate ways.

Defence Counsel: Go on.

Kurt Wolfson: I went out to the woods around four and helped build the bonfire. It was hot, so I grabbed a couple of beers and waited for the party to start.

Defence Counsel: Do you remember meeting Miss Scarlett?

Kurt Wolfson: Yeah. She arrived with her hot cheerleader friend about seven.

Defence Counsel: Did you know Emily Scarlett prior to this meeting?

Kurt Wolfson: She went to my high school, so I'd seen her around. I had never spoken to her before.

Defence Counsel: Just to be clear, you had never spoken to Emily Scarlett before the night of May 27th, 2017?

Kurt Wolfson: No. Why would I? She wore glasses and was kind of nerdy. She wasn't my type.

Defence Counsel: Tell us in your own words what happened when you met Miss Scarlett on that night.

Kurt Wolfson: She and her friend Cindy showed up about seven. I found them in the bathroom and went to say hello.

Defence Counsel: The bathroom?

Kurt Wolfson: Yeah. We had filled the bathtub full of ice to keep the drinks cold.

Defence Counsel: And by drinks you mean alcohol, is that correct?

Kurt Wolfson: Yeah.

Defence Counsel: So had you been drinking on this particular night?

Kurt Wolfson: Yeah. I had a couple of beers already by this point. Why wouldn't I? We were celebrating. It had been a great year. I won us the state championship for the third year running and we'd just graduated.

Judge: I saw that game. Excellent teamwork. Well played, son.

Kurt Wolfson: Thanks, Your Honour.

District Attorney: Objection!

Judge: Overruled. Go on, son.

Kurt Wolfson: Normally, Emily was all buttoned up at school. You know, walking around with her nose in a book. But that night she looked different. She was in this tight little red dress and she looked hot. I could tell by the way she bent over the bathtub to grab a beer that she wanted to hook up.

Distract Attorney: Objection! Speculation! The witness can't know what was Miss Scarlett was thinking.

Judge: Overruled. The boy is allowed to express an opinion. Continue.

Kurt Wolfson: So a couple hours later I saw her wandering away from the bonfire. She turned around and sort of waved at me.

Defence Counsel: So she was beckoning you to follow?

District Attorney: Objection! Calls for speculation.

Judge: Overruled. The boy can say what he thought she was indicating. Proceed.

Kurt Wolfson: She waved at me to follow her, so I knew that she wanted me.

Defence Counsel: Go on.

Kurt Wolfson: I caught up with her and we started walking away from the party. She tripped over a tree root and fell down on her knees. You know, like doggy style. She laughed because her knee was bleeding and said she was clumsy, but I could tell she'd done it on purpose so I would look at her ass.

District Attorney: Objection again, Your Honour! The witness cannot know what Miss Scarlett was thinking.

Judge: Again you are overruled. It is pretty clear to me what she was suggesting.

Defence Counsel: What did you do next?

Kurt Wolfson: I rolled her on her back, and we started kissing.

Defence Counsel: And you are certain that was mutual, that you were not forcing yourself on her in any way?

Kurt Wolfson: Absolutely. She was really into it. You could tell. She was kissing me back and she had wrapped her legs around me.

Defence Counsel: You had sexual intercourse with her that night did you not?

Kurt Wolfson: Yeah, I did. But it wasn't rape. She wanted me as much as I wanted her.

Defence Counsel: Thank you Mr Wolfson. Your witness.

District Attorney: You said the sexual intercourse was a mutual decision is that right?

Kurt Wolfson: Yeah.

District Attorney: And how did you know that she gave her consent? Did you ask her permission before you penetrated her?

Kurt Wolfson: No. If she had wanted me to stop, she would have said so.

District Attorney: But was she incapable of asking you to stop?

Kurt Wolfson: Do you mean was she drunk? We were all drunk. It was a party.

District Attorney: Exhibit B, Your Honour. The blood alcohol level of Emily Scarlett when she was examined by medical staff at CarolinaEast Medical Centre. You will see it is recorded at 0.22% which is high enough to cause blackouts. Mr Wolfson, you said earlier that Miss Scarlett tripped over a tree root and fell, is that correct?

Kurt Wolfson: Yeah. She fell and tore up her knee.

District Attorney: Did you do anything to help Miss Scarlett?

Kurt Wolfson: She didn't need any help. She was laughing about it and said it didn't even hurt.

District Attorney: Did she complain about blurred vision being the cause of her fall?

Kurt Wolfson: No. She just said she was clumsy.

District Attorney: So, while she was bleeding profusely from the knee you rolled her over and began to kiss her. Is that correct?

Kurt Wolfson: She wasn't bothered by it, so why should I have been?

District Attorney: What happened next?

Kurt Wolfson: I banged her.

District Attorney: And by "banged her" you mean you engaged in sexual intercourse?

Kurt Wolfson: Yeah.

District Attorney: Was this before or after you bludgeoned her in the head?

Defence Counsel: Objection! Argumentative!

Judge: I will not have that kind of talk in my courtroom without proof.

District Attorney: But there is proof Your Honour. Emily Scarlett's medical records show—

Judge: Yes, that she hit her head somehow, but not that this young man did it. Change direction Counsellor.

District Attorney: I will rephrase the question. Emily Scarlett had a large lump on her head and was diagnosed with a concussion in the hospital. Do you know anything about how she sustained this injury?

Kurt Wolfson: When I was banging her, I was going pretty hard. Her head was knocking up against the tree trunk.

District Attorney: Her head was repeatedly banging up against the tree and yet you didn't stop?

Kurt Wolfson: No. I was really into it.

District Attorney: Did Miss Scarlett complain?

Kurt Wolfson: No. She wasn't saying anything by that point.

District Attorney: And why was that Mr Wolfson?

Kurt Wolfson: She had passed out.

District Attorney: She had passed out and yet you continued to have intercourse with her?

Kurt Wolfson: Yeah. I wasn't finished.

District Attorney: What happened after you "finished"?

Kurt Wolfson: She woke up a bit.

District Attorney: She woke up. Did she speak to you?

Kurt Wolfson: Yeah. She asked me to do some other stuff to her.

District Attorney: What sort of requests did she make of you?

Kurt Wolfson: I couldn't believe it. She had always seemed like such a goody two shoes.

District Attorney: I will ask you again, what request did she make of you?

Kurt Wolfson: She asked me to do anal.

District Attorney: And by "anal" you mean anal intercourse. Is that correct?

Kurt Wolfson: Yeah. She asked me to do her with a tree branch.

District Attorney: Just to be clear, she asked you to sodomise her with a tree branch?

Kurt Wolfson: Yeah. That's what she said.

District Attorney: And what were her exact words?

Kurt Wolfson: She said, "A stick's going up my butt."

District Attorney: And you took this to mean she wanted you to insert a tree branch in her anus?

Kurt Wolfson: Yeah. She was really up for it. She said it three times before she passed out again.

District Attorney: Did it ever occur to you she might have been complaining that she was uncomfortable because she was lying on the ground and there was a branch under her body?

Defence Counsel: Objection! Calls for speculation.

District Attorney: I'll withdraw the question, Your Honour. Mr Wolfson, can you tell the court what happened next?

Kurt Wolfson: I was tackled by Stubby and Perky.

District Attorney: By Stubby and Perky you mean Charles Stubbins and Lionel Perkins. Is that correct?

Kurt Wolfson: Yeah. I couldn't believe it. I thought they were my friends.

District Attorney: Did they tell you why they tackled you?

Kurt Wolfson: Yeah. They said I was a "sick bastard" for doing that to Emily when she was unconscious.

District Attorney: No further questions.

Peter, Peter, Pumpkin Eater

Peter, Peter, pumpkin eater,
Had a wife and couldn't keep her;
He put her in a pumpkin shell,
And there he kept her very well.

Peter, Peter, Husband, King,
Pumpkin eater, wedding ring,
Wife beater, jealous thing.
Poor child, just fourteen.

Peter, Peter, had a wife
Who lived in fear and had no life.
A wisp of girl, so young and slight.
Oftentimes she cried at night.

Peter, Peter, couldn't keep her.
Stupid wench. He used a wrench.
He put her in a pumpkin shell.
Made her life a living Hell
And there he kept her very well.

Author's note: *All my life I have been intrigued by this nursery rhyme. Supposedly in Colonial America the word "pumpkin" was a euphemism for a woman's genitalia and some scholars believe that a "pumpkin shell" refers to a chastity belt. I also read on slang dictionary lingomash.com that "pumpkin eater" is a word currently used to mean a paedophile who desires young boys under the age of consent. I have not included either of those ideas in this particular poem, but rather stuck with the image that I held from my childhood—that of a battered young wife and her domineering older husband.*

Not Waving, but Drowning

Dear Diary,

It's me. Ariel. We go way back you and me. Well, not you exactly. I chose you special for The Event. But having a diary. A non-judgmental trusted friend. You alone know how much I adore stationery. All those beautiful books just aching to be written in with a fancy pen. I've been writing in you in one form or another since I was thirteen. But the person reading this, you won't know this about me. You don't know me at all. You'll be surprised when you read it here in my diary. And you will be reading my diary because I will be leaving it on the beach for you to find. You can call it my note if you like. It's my explanation. That's for you mom because you always need a reason. When you read this, and you will read this, you will pore over it

76

looking for signs and there won't be any. Not ones you could find. Because you never really knew me.

The first question you want to ask me is did I know him? Of course I did. Who doesn't know Roy Prince? He's a surfer. No wait. He's king of the surfers. The real question is did he know me? The answer to that is a big fat no. Emphasis on fat. No. Roy Prince the Surf God did not know Ariel Ursula Priest the geek. He never knew I existed until I dyed my hair.

Over the Thanksgiving holiday I visited my cousin in San Diego. She's a beautician. She said coloured hair was all the rage. Not like red or brown or black. But blue and green and purple. She said my hair was a perfect canvas because of the colour. My mom always says my hair is the colour of dirty dishwater, but I think it's more like the colour of a cardboard box. Anyway, I let her do it and suddenly I looked amazing. The colours looked like the sky and the sea all at once. If you are looking at my hair, you'll be distracted so you won't notice my big ass. That's what I hoped anyway.

When I came back to the shithole that is Encinitas, I was the only one with The Hair. That's how he noticed me. I was sitting on the seawall secretly watching him while pretending to read No Exit by Jean Paul Sartre. He walked by with his cronies and they made the usual remarks. I will not defile this diary by writing what they said. But they said it often. Every time they saw me. He stopped though and looked at me. I will say that again. He. Looked. At. Me. He reached out his hand and gave my hair a playful tug. You look like a mermaid. That's what he said. A mermaid. Then he walked off.

Diary—I thought I'd died. That was the pinnacle of my miserable experience. I was touched by a boy. Not a boy. A God. And he thought I looked like a mermaid.

On Monday at school I saw him. His locker is by mine. We're assigned alphabetically. Priest. Prince. We've had lockers by each other since junior high. We've had adjacent lockers for six years and he never once NOT ONCE spoke to me. But that day he did. Hey mermaid he said. And then walked off. He had spoken to me twice. TWICE in three days. I thought if I died right there my life would be complete. Can it get better than this?

Yes it can. On Tuesday he called out Hey mermaid wait up. He wanted to know if he could look at my English homework as he hadn't read any of Macbeth and didn't know what Mrs H was talking about in class. Of course I said. I'd gladly give him my homework every day. Cool he said. Thanks mermaid. And he patted me on the ass. I will say that again. He. Patted. Me. On. The. Ass!!!!!!!! Me. He touched me. In a sexual way. Big Ass Ariel. Oh God I swore I wasn't going to write that down. But it doesn't matter. None of it matters. He touched me.

On Wednesday as I was giving him my English homework, he said What are you doing on Friday night mermaid? My throat was so dry it was like I had eaten sandpaper. I did this little cough thing to clear my throat and I saw him frown a bit, so I just found my voice and said all casual like, well nothing I couldn't cancel. What would you like to do? He laughed, and I suddenly thought Oh God Ariel he was not asking you out, you big blobby idiot. He was just asking. I blushed like a fire truck and tried to run away, but my locker door was still open, and I ran face first into it. That made him laugh even harder. Like holding his sides sort of laughing. I prayed that a big hole would open up in the floor and swallow me. But it didn't. Instead he put his hand on my shoulder and said Why not. Let me see what you got mermaid.

On Thursday he said it was a pain to have to copy my homework, so over lunch I did my English assignment twice. I did my best to imitate his handwriting and I made sure to get a few wrong on my assignment so it didn't look like we had copied each other. I knew Mrs H was going to notice because English is my best subject, but I can't look like I'm smarter than him. Once I heard him say to Helen Dooley that girls can be too smart for their own good. He hated the way she raised her hand all the time trying to make everyone else look stupid. He said she was a speccy four eyes. It made her cry. But it was her fault. She reminded Mrs H that we were supposed to have a quiz on The Scarlet Letter. He was just mad because he hadn't had time to study. I know he didn't mean it. Like I once heard him say to his friends that men seldom make passes at girls with fat asses as he pointed in my direction. And I had a date with him on Friday, so it can't be true.

On Friday he asked me to meet him at the mall. He had to get a ride with his older brother, so he didn't know exactly what time he'd get there. I said I was happy to wait. He said we could go see a movie. Some sort of teen comedy with lots of sex and underage drinking. Then he winked at me. Winked!! I said I would be at the movie theatre for the 5:30 showing. I lied and said I had period cramps so I could check out of school early and spent the afternoon getting ready. I washed and dried my mermaid hair. I put on this dress I had been saving for just this sort of an occasion. It was a dress that made me look at bit like a chunky version of Stevie Nicks from a Fleetwood Mac album that my mom bought at a flea market. The dress was white and floaty and had all these ribbons on it. It made me look like a bride crossed with a butterfly. I wasn't dumb enough to think Roy Prince would see me and want to marry me (We were only seniors. There was plenty of time for getting serious after college.) but I hoped that when he saw me it would take his breath away.

I got to the mall and waited. And waited. And waited. I was fighting back tears when the Surf God turned up. Sorry he said. It's fine I said. I didn't mind. I brought a book in my purse to pass the time. I saw him do that frown again so I slid my copy of Angela Carter's The Bloody Chamber back into my bag. I stood up and did a little twirl. He took off his jacket and wrapped it around my shoulders. How sweet! Such a gentleman. The mall is notoriously freezing. It's like living inside an Orange Julius. I smiled, and he said I just don't want anybody to see you in that ridiculous outfit. Jesus, where you dig that up? 1970? I did not know until that moment that it was possible for a fat person to shrink. But I do now. We got to the counter and asked for two tickets. He said I should pay for this and he'd get us something from McDonalds after. It used all the money that I had been saving, but I didn't care. He must have noticed that I was a feminist since I was reading Angela Carter and would want to pay my share. Going Dutch my mom called it. It meant that he saw us as equals.

The theatre got dark and we settled in to watch the movie about the geeky kids all trying to get laid. After about 20 minutes I felt his hand on my thigh. He was slowly easing up my skirt and I wasn't sure what I should do. I sort of thought he'd kiss me first, but these days relationships are different. Or so it says in Seventeen magazine. I felt his hand slide up my thigh and into my panties. I will say that again. OMG! He. Fingered. Me!!!!! My body felt like it had been zapped with 1000 volts of electricity and he touched me on the place that I thought only I knew about. I was afraid I was going to scream from the deliciousness of it all, but suddenly just when it started to get good, he slid his finger out and wiped it on his jeans. He didn't touch me for the rest of the movie which was a huge disappointment. I guess he realised he was moving too fast. The movie ended up being quite funny. There was a scene in an aquarium that made me laugh so much I snorted. Shhh he said. Shut up or someone will hear you. I looked at my lap for the rest of the movie and didn't make a sound. A good girlfriend does not embarrass her boyfriend out in public.

After the film I was starving. Literally starving. I hadn't eaten since breakfast. I skipped lunch to come home and get ready for the date. I was trying to be as quiet as possible so he wouldn't get mad again, but my stomach kept making this noise like an eighteen wheeler. We left the mall and walked across the street to Micky D's. He took off without me and I had a terrible time catching up with him as I was wearing heels. By the time I got there he was sitting at a table with some of his friends. How was the movie they sniggered. Shut up he said and gave one of them a shove. Can we get something to eat please I said. A Big Mac and some fries and a large coke if that's OK. I'm starving. He looked at me and then swatted me on the backside. You don't need all that fat, baby. Just get a coke. Make it a diet coke. One of his friends started to laugh, but I didn't care. He likes me. He said so. He called me his baby. He gave me a dollar and I went to get a diet coke. When I was at the machine getting a refill, I heard him say that when he tried to finger me it was like a jungle down there. It was disgusting. He liked his girls skinny and smooth. I sat at the edge of the table carefully sipping my third diet coke while he and his friends high fived each other. I was thinking about where I was going to get the money for some hair removal cream since I had spent all my allowance on movie tickets.

Luckily, I found some new razors under the bathroom sink and so on Saturday I decided to shave everything off. I mean everything. I wanted to be perfectly smooth for him. I wanted to be the kind of girl he likes. I mean, he's right. The dress was a mistake. I don't want to get the reputation of being some sort of crazy hippy and I could stand to lose a pound or two (or twenty or thirty). I decided to make a self-improvement list. I went to my stationery drawer (Yes, I have a stationery drawer. Doesn't everyone?) and pulled out a brand new book with a lilac cover and a unicorn. I decided to write all the things that I needed to do to make Roy keep liking me. I mean, he does like me. He wouldn't have asked me out or tried to finger me if he didn't. But I want him to love me. And for that I have to be different.

On Monday I left a note in his locker that said I shaved down there and drew a little heart with an arrow pointing down. He came to me at lunch to get his homework and said Shaved, huh. You know what I like. My parents are out tonight. Wanna come over and let me try out that new shaved pussy of yours? I said yes. Of course I said yes. It was longest conversation we had ever had. He was probably expecting me to sleep with him, but I knew I wasn't ready. I had read about heavy petting in Seventeen magazine and I figured we could try some of that, but what I really wanted was for him to kiss me. I wanted my first kiss to be him because he was my soul mate.

After school I had to shave down below again as it was all stubbly and itchy and I didn't want to ruin the moment having to scratch down there. Mom was working late again (no surprise there) and so I left her a note that said I was going out to a meeting about my big presentation for French class next week. More like big presentation of French kissing. At least I hoped it would be. I also said I had eaten which was obviously a lie because I was on a diet again, but she didn't need to know that. She'd only start the Oh Ariel 130 pounds is not fat song and dance routine again. I know what I am. I am the biggest girl in the senior class. I am a whale. But not for long.

When I arrived at his house, he was playing a video game. When he finished, he took me to his bedroom and turned on his computer to play some music. I think it was Eminem. This was it. I had been so careful how I dressed. No weird stuff. Just jeans and a tee shirt. Normal clothes. Clothes he likes. Here was where he was going to tenderly take me in his arms and stroke my mermaid hair. He would carefully remove my glasses and then gently kiss me. But that's not what happened.

Instead he unzipped his jeans and his thing uncoiled like an enormous snake. It was as big around as a coke can. On my life I swear that's true. You wanna show me how much you like me mermaid he said. Then suck me off. So I did.

It was not quite the romantic evening I had imagined. It was harder to give a blowjob than I thought it would be and my jaw ached. I wanted to be one of those snakes that I read about in National Geographic that could unhinge their lower jaw to swallow bigger prey. It was all getting a bit too much, but it's hard to say that with your mouth full. I tried to pull away, but he increased the pressure on the back of my head and kept shoving his thing into my mouth. I had a brief moment where I thought I was drowning. Like I couldn't breathe, and I would suffocate. At the inquest they would say How did she die, and the answer would be Suffocation by thingy. It was making my nose run and I snotted all over him, but he didn't seem to notice thankfully. Suddenly he tightened his grip on my hair and I felt his gunk fill my mouth. He pushed too far into the back of my throat and hit my uvula. That was a mistake because I have a very strong gag reflex. I coughed up a little bit of puke onto his pants and he pushed me away. Jesus mermaid. Go clean yourself up.

I went to the bathroom and I looked like a crazy woman. There was vomit on my chin and my nose was boiling over with snot. Apparently, it had made my eyes water quite a bit and my mascara (which falsely claimed to be waterproof) had run down my face making me look like a sad panda. I washed up as best as I could and smoothed my mermaid hair down. I went back to his bedroom, but he was already downstairs. He was playing a video game again. I sat down on the edge of the sofa and waited for my turn. I had shaved just for him. When would it be my go? I waited. And waited. And waited. Finally it was nearly eleven and I had to get home. I stood up to leave and he called my name. Mermaid he said. Don't forget we have an English test tomorrow. If I need help, you'll give me it to me. Right?

As I walked home, I reflected on what had been my second sexual experience if you counted the ten seconds of fingering at the movie theatre. (Which I did.) It was great. He enjoyed it. I mean, he finished. He came. That was good. I made that happen. Me. Ariel Ursula Priest made that happen. You can't do that if you don't love the other person just a little, right? He just wants to take turns, I thought. Next time will be my turn again.

The next day I carefully got dressed. Nothing too strange. A button-down shirt and jeans. I walked into school and I heard a few people laughing. That's what they do. People laugh when I go by. Fat Ariel the weirdo. That's me. But not anymore. I was going out with the king of our school. The coolest surfer in the county. We had been on two dates and done sexual stuff and from now on my life was going to be different. As I walked through the halls towards my locker the laughter got louder. People were openly pointing at me. Something was wrong. I got to my locker and he was there. He had his back to me, but I could hear every word he said about how he had won $100 from his friends. After that day at the seawall they had bet him that he couldn't get me to have sex with him. But there had to be proof. When he turned on his computer, he had also turned on his webcam and he had filmed the whole thing. It had streamed live, and everyone saw. They saw everything. They saw me.

I went through the rest of the day like a clam. I closed myself up tight in my shell. I ignored all the voices around me that were saying Suck it, Ariel and making gagging noises. I ignored all the whispers. I held my head high, but when he asked me for the answers to the test, I pretended I couldn't hear him.

I walked home and let myself in. Mom had left me a note saying she had dinner with a client so don't wait up. I left her a note saying I was going down to the sea to collect some stones for a school project. I reached into my stationery drawer and pulled out the most beautiful book that I had been saving for a special occasion. This book. My last book. It has a big heart made of satin on the front because it was going to be the book that I wrote about love. About my soulmate.

I took it down to the shore and sat on the seawall. I wrote...am writing...about the fact that I do not have a soulmate. I never did. I understand that now. I hope he chokes on every dime he spends. I hope that my death will poison the sea and he will fall off his surfboard with every wave he tries to ride. With any luck he'll be eaten by a shark.

I am going to leave this here on the seawall to be found by some innocent passer-by. Perhaps you are the person who has found the book and is frantically scanning the horizon to see if you can see me not waving but drowning. But you won't. I filled my pockets with stones and when I walk into the arms of the sea I will not be coming out.

To my mother: it wouldn't have made a difference if you had been home. I would have ended up in the sea sooner or later. That's what happens to soulless folks like me.

So with this I bid you so long, farewell, auf wiedersehen, goodnight and all that cliché rot. Goodbye to all those who never tried to get to know me. Perhaps you are soulless too.

Ariel

Pink Workplace Blues

Little boy blue
talks over you.
Won't let you get a word in.
Steals your ideas then mansplains them to
you and he gets a promotion
with more money, too.

Little girl pink
with a leer and a wink,
Don't be so frigid, my dear.
Be a good sport and do as you're told
or you'll lose your job
and be out in the cold.

The Trial of Emily Scarlett, part 3

Bailiff: All rise. Superior Court of the state of North Carolina is now in session, the honourable Judge Hunter presiding. Please be seated.

Judge: Ladies and gentlemen of the jury, have you reached a unanimous verdict?

Jury Foreman: We have, Your Honour.

Judge: On the first count of rape of an intoxicated person, how do you find?

Jury Foreman: Your Honour, we find the defendant, Kurt Wolfson, guilty.

Judge: On the second count of rape of an unconscious person, how do you find?

Jury Foreman: We find the defendant guilty.

Judge: On the third count of sexually penetrating an intoxicated person with a foreign object, how do you find?

Jury Foreman: We find the defendant guilty.

Judge: On the fourth count of sexually penetrating an unconscious person with a foreign object, how do you find?

Jury Foreman: We find the defendant guilty.

Judge: Thank you. You may be seated. Now I have listened to the arguments of this trial and it is time for me to decide on the sentence Kurt Wolfson deserves. The District Attorney thinks he should get a six-year sentence in state prison saying the boy lacks remorse and that his victim was especially vulnerable in her unconscious state. But I say different. Kurt Wolfson is a fine upstanding boy. I have followed his football career at Forest Hills High School, and he is a hero to many a young boy out there. We have heard testimony from Pastor Jim Duplis from First Baptist Church and football coach Norm

Moran attesting to his good character. The boy has no criminal history. Yes, alcohol was involved and may have impaired his judgement, but a boy like that deserves to let off steam after the year he has had on the football field. The fact is, there was a drunk girl in a short red dress flirting with him by a bonfire. What else was the boy supposed to think? Any red-blooded American boy would have done the same.

I have considered the consequences of prison and it is obvious that a prison sentence would have a severe impact on a boy like Kurt Wolfson who has such a bright future ahead of him. It would be a crime to ruin this boy's life for twenty minutes of action. I will be speaking to the dean of Duke University to get this boy's football scholarship reinstated so that he may attend and bring glory to God and to my alma mater. Therefore, I hereby sentence you, Kurt Stephen Wolfson, to six months in the county jail and three years of probation. Court is adjourned.

Quite Contrary

Mister Blue, who hasn't got a clue,
Why does his business grow?
Because he's assertive, decisive and
a strategic leader who is confident,
ambitious and commanding.
That's why his business grows.

Lady Ms Pink, who knows how to think,
Why won't her business grow?
Because she's aggressive, bossy and
a manipulative controller who is arrogant,
ambitious and pushy.
That's why her business won't grow.

Author's note: *I read an interesting article in Harvard Business Review that talked about how the same traits in men and women were often perceived very differently, The identical behaviour was seen as positive for a man (decisive), but negative for a woman (bossy). The article also said that in adulthood the word ambitious was an insult for women but not for men.*

The Call of the Owl

With some considerable difficulty, the old man pulled on his fur lined boots and coat and trudged outside to find a piece of wood. Their little hut, deep in the heart of the forest, was a wedding cake frosted with snow. He surveyed the fallen branches and found a suitable candidate for whittling. The branch was almost as thick as his arm. It would serve its purpose. He came back to his front door and as he was shaking the snow from his boots, he heard the call of the owl. It made him shiver. He closed the door.

The old woman had been standing over the iron stove and was listlessly stirring the soup.

"Where did you go?" she asked, not looking at him.

"You know where I went, Mama. To do what must be done." He did not look at her either.

She continued to stir the soup, but her shoulders shook with grief. The old man sat down in his chair beside the fire and pulled out his knife and began to strip the bark off of the branch.

"Did you hear the owl?" he asked softly to the rhythmic scraping of metal on wood. She did not answer, keeping her back firmly to the old man so he would not see her tears.

"Mama, did you hear it call? It is a sign. It must be done tonight."

Suddenly the old woman turned, spoon in hand.

"Papa, what if you are wrong?" She chose her words carefully. "What if she is not... infected?"

On the last word, she thrust the spoon towards the old man like a dagger.

"She is contaminated, and you know it Mama. Add more garlic to the soup."

Dutifully she did so, pulling each clove from the bulb and smashing it with the spoon and then peeling the papery skin away. She tossed the cloves in the pot. There was no need to chop them. Not for this. The old man brushed away the bark shavings from his lap and grimly began to whittle. The old woman walked around the tiny kitchen and tamped the dried herbs she had strewn on the floor. Papa had insisted on protective herbs.

The sound of a wolf howling to the full moon startled her. She turned to her husband who was making a sharp point to his stick.

"Ivan is not back yet. What if he is eaten by the wolf?" Her eyes pleaded with him to understand; she could not lose another child.

"You know we had no choice but to send Ivan to the village. He will not be eaten. He has more sense than to dally in the woods under the moon."

This time he did look at the old woman, piercing her with his gaze to remind her of what happened. As if she would ever forget.

It had been exactly a month. It was a night like this one, a cold clear night with a full moon. Nathalia had been restless all day, pleading to go the village, but they kept clear of the village as much as they could. "We keep ourselves to ourselves," Papa had told her. Nathalia flounced about the tiny hut with indignation and then took herself off to her room. That night, something possessed her. They never understood what it was, but Mama suspected she was having a clandestine meeting in the woods with Rolf from the village. He, too, made many excuses to come out to their hut isolated among so many trees. Whatever it was, she went out that fateful night. She went out into the snow and when she was found it was clear that something terrible had happened. She was defiled. She was unclean.

It was the owl that had woken Papa. The owl screeching loudly had woken him and he gazed out the frosted window and that is when he saw her, his Nathalia, lying in the snow. Her nightdress was torn and there was blood, so much blood. He woke Mama and they both rushed out to bring her inside. Despite having lain in the snow for some time, her body was not cold. It was hot. Feverish. She burned and she would not wake. Mama and Ivan sponged her body with cold water in an effort to bring down the fever while Papa rushed to the village to accuse Rolf of misdeeds, but his family were away and so whoever or whatever had attacked his daughter was a mystery.

For a month, she had lain in bed. Feverishly she tossed and turned. Sometimes she cried out, but she would not wake. It was then that the old man began to suspect. He checked her over and found the mark. It was hidden on her body in a secret place, but it was the mark of evil he had no doubt. The old woman tried to convince him it was a birthmark, but he knew evil when he saw it. It must be done.

They both began the rhythm of their activities once again, him sharpening the wooden stick into a point and her stirring more garlic into the soup. They were so absorbed in their activities as they waited for

Ivan's return that they did not hear her open the door.

Nathalia was standing in the doorway wearing her white nightdress and her hair was as red as a fox's tail. She was thin, almost weightless, and she glided softly into the kitchen and reached out and put her hand on her mother's hunched shoulder. Her mother leapt away as if she had been scalded and the spoon clattered to the ground.

"Mama, why so jumpy?" the ghostly girl queried. Her mother stood open mouthed, trembling as her daughter stepped towards her.

"Stay back!" she cried as she pulled the Rosary from her apron pocket and started to pray. The girl didn't seem to notice. She danced around the kitchen, bringing up the dust of the dried herbs. By now the father was watching as well.

"Mama, why have you put the herbs on the floor? Silly sausage! I shall have to get the broom and help you clean up after dinner."

The parents stared at their daughter, who looked virtually unchanged from a month ago. Considerably thinner, but everything else was the same. How could that be? She had lain unconscious, but still breathing, for a month. She had looked so different lying in the bed that they had called the Priest to administer last rites and he had advised them what to do. Now this. Here she was as young and fresh as she had been before the attack. It made the mother less sure, but it made the father more certain.

The girl seemed amused by their bewilderment. She yawned and stretched like a cat, showing her ribs through her thin gown. "I'm so hungry, Mama! I feel as though I haven't eaten in weeks!" Her father turned away and continued to sharpen the wood.

"What are you doing Papa? Are you carving another solider for Ivan? It is the wrong shape; the head is much too pointy." She reached out to lightly touch the end and he recoiled slightly.

"By the way, where is my little brother?" she asked.

"We sent him to fetch the—" her mother began.

"We sent him to fetch some wood for the fire. That is right, is it not Mama?" His gaze impaled her heart and she turned back to the soup.

"Mama, that soup smells delicious. May I have a bowl, please?" The mother looked to the father for guidance and he nodded, so she filled a bowl with the soup and laid it before the girl who used to be their daughter. Who might still be their daughter. The girl ate the soup in silence except for the occasional slurp and then pronounced, "You were a bit heavy on the garlic Mama. My breath will stink for a week. What will Rolf say when he tries to kiss me?"

The mention of Rolf made her toss her vixen mane and laugh.

"Do you remember the last full moon? I heard the call of the owl and thought it might have been Rolf. That was our secret signal. I put on my boots and I went outside to look for him, but I could not see him. It was freezing and so I quickly came back inside and went back to bed. Do you remember that night? I caught a terrible cold from being outside and was in bed for a month!"

The mother was mouthing the Hail Mary as the Rosary flowed through her hands like water. Perhaps it had all been a mistake. She looked to her husband who was leaning back in the chair with his eyes closed, still clutching the wooden stake. Suddenly he spoke, but without opening his eyes.

"Go to your room Nathalia. We do not want to hear about your sordid goings on with Rolf."

Just like the old days the daughter flounced off in a huff and slammed her door. The mother quickly rushed to the father's side.

"Papa! See, she is not infected! She ate the garlic soup! She did not try to harm us! She has just been unwell! Perhaps it was just—"

"The soup proves nothing. The herbs protected us. It still must be done."

There was a light knocking on the door and the old man wearily pushed himself up out of the chair and went to answer it. Shivering on the doorstep were his son Ivan and the Priest.

"Is she still showing signs of infection?" the Priest asked.

"No!" cried the mother.

"Yes!" cried the father.

"But she woke up! She came out and spoke to us and ate my garlic soup. She is not contagious. Please—"

"She woke up and spoke to you?" the Priest replied. "This is most serious. It must be done immediately."

The wife, who followed her husband in all things was crying as she pulled on her fur lined boots and coat. As soon as everyone was dressed, they walked out of the house and the husband locked the door. The Priest painted a cross on the door with a chalky white liquid.

"What is the cross for?" Ivan asked.

The Priest replied, "It means the house is under quarantine. No one should go in or out until it is safe. Tonight, you and your family will sleep in the church in the village. Tomorrow morning your father and I will come back and take care of the infection. Then it will be safe to return." He smiled at the boy and patted his head. Disinfecting was always hard on a family. Particularly the mothers.

As they lumbered their way through the blanket of snow towards the lights of the village, they heard the call of the owl. Ivan turned and saw the pale face of his sister staring sadly out of the window. He turned back and twined his arms with that of his Mama and Papa. He did not look back again.

16

By the Pricking of My Thumb
(The Beauty Sleeps)

After I was pricked at sixteen,
I began to sleep through life.
A trance (of sorts)
I used words like thorns to keep boys at bay,
but still my prickly nature did not hide
my beauty.
They came (one after the other)
demanding what was theirs by right.
They had earned it (earned me?)
by slicing through the bindweed that
strangled my heart.
Everyone took their turn
to try to wake me up from my slumber.
(Sleeping somehow implies consent.)
If you don't struggle it hurts less
and is over quicker.
I never said yes, but I never say no.

Home From the Sea

His earliest memory was of his mother turning out his room. She said in her heavily accented English, "It is not enough to clean the surfaces. You must get underneath everything and see what might be hidden."

There was a foreignness to his mother. She was not like other boys' mothers. She had come from across the sea.

The boy looked nothing like his father. He lacked the disapproving features that his father habitually wore. He shared his mother's changeable eyes—one minute blue, the next minute greenish-grey.

"Stormy eyes," she told him. "Like the sea."

He had never seen the ocean. His father wouldn't allow it. They had once lived by the coast. He was born there, but he did not remember it at all. When he was a baby, his father decided to move them to heart of the city.

"It was for your mother's health," the father always said. "She was obsessed with the sea. I needed her to be a proper wife and a mother to you. She couldn't do that if she was always trying to drown herself."

"I wasn't trying to drown myself," the mother whispered. "I just wanted to go home."

His father worked in the city. He often travelled for work. He would pack everything in his special travelling bag and be gone for several days at a time. It was during those times that his mother would tear up the house searching for something.

"I need my fur coat," she always said. The boy could not understand why she needed a new coat. Hadn't the father bought her that splendid wool one only last year? Her misty eyes would hold back tears. He brought her comfort the only way he knew how. He made her a cup of hot water with a pinch of salt. It was her favourite drink.

He seemed instinctively to understand that it would anger his father if he knew that the mother desired a new coat, so he kept silent. Together they kept many secrets from the father.

Every day that his father was away working in the city, he and his mother would take the bus into town and go to the fishmongers. She knew every kind of fish in the sea it seemed. Each day, they would buy some fish for their midday meal. She would cook it for them, and they ate it in silence. She closed her eyes as she ate.

"This is what the sea tastes like," she would murmur. It was a special treat, just for the two of them. A meal only for those with stormy eyes. Her father had forbidden them to eat fish.

"Too much like the sea for my taste," he grunted. "Too fishy."

"But shouldn't fish be fishy, father?" the boy asked timidly.

"How would you know? You've never eaten the stuff. Meat. That's what men like us need. Meat."

The boy saw his mother's eyes change from blue to grey and he knew he must keep silent on the matter. In the evening, she cooked meat for them all, but whenever they could, they enjoyed the fish together. He longed for the taste of the sea.

The mother told him wondrous stories, but only when the father was not around. Her descriptions were so vivid that he felt he knew exactly what it was like to crunch sand between his toes, to feel the warmth of the sun on his shoulders as the briny waves crashed about his feet. He delighted in the tales about shoals of fish swimming beneath the surface of the clear, blue water. In the bath, he pretended to be a fish, but it was not the same. He longed to swim in the sea.

When he started school at the age of six, he learned to read quickly because his mother had taught him his letters. A is for algae, B is for bladderwrack, C is for carp. One day after she picked him up from school, she took him to a bookshop. It was there that she bought him a copy of a marvellous book entitled "The Little Mermaid." Here, finally, were drawings of the sea! It was even more beautiful than the mother had described. His heart felt so light that he thought it might fly out of his chest. His father felt differently. He wrenched the book from the boy's hands and threw it on the fire. The boy watched as the beautiful paintings curled and distorted. The room was a cascade of colour. His face hot and red with tears, his mother pale and trembling, and the father purple with rage.

"I have told you time and again, not to fill that boy's head with nonsense, have I not?" he snarled. She simply nodded.

"There is nothing for you by the sea. Do you understand, boy? The sea is where little boys like you DROWN!" The boy was terrified. His mother had only spoken of a sea that brought peace and contentment. She had never mentioned a sea that brought death.

"I've been away too often with travel," the father pondered. "The boy has had too much time with you. Too much of your influence. I think it is time we did something about that, don't you?"

And so it was that at the tender age of seven, the boy was sent away to boarding school in the heart of another city, far away from the sea. He grew, as boys often do, into a replica of his father. This happens when boys are guided by stern men and denied tenderness. It was precisely what the father hoped for; it was exactly what the mother feared.

The boy dutifully returned home every holiday. With each visit, he had less and less time for his mother and her foolish fantasies. He and his father talked way into the night about the joys of business. He planned to follow in his father's footsteps and work in the city. He would get a wife and son of his own. One night after he and his father had consumed more whiskey than they should, he told his father about the searches his mother used to make when he was travelling. The father exploded with laughter which led to a coughing fit. After much pounding on his back by the boy, he got his breath back and muttered, "She'll ne'er find it while I am alive." The boy did not know what his father meant, but he laughed all the same. He laughed at all the wasted years that his mother had searched. He laughed at her foolishness. She sat upstairs and silently cried.

The boy, who was now a man, came back for his father's funeral. It had been many years since he had returned to that house in the heart of the city. He had a similar house in the heart of a nearby city, and he was busy with his own wife and son and work. Too busy to look in on his aging mother. His mother looked ancient. Faded. Like something bleached by the sun. He assumed it was the shock of his father's death. Hadn't she been devoted to him? She sat there on the sofa drinking a cup of hot, salty water. He had forgotten she did that. *Daft old thing,* he mused to himself. *She always was a fool.*

There was much to do. Clear away his father's clothes, for a start. Some of his suits were still perfectly good and it would be a shame to waste them. He grabbed his father's travelling bag and began to pack. As his hand reached into the depths of the bag, he noticed that there was a false bottom to it. He lifted the hinge and his hand felt something strange. Almost furry. He pulled it out and it was some sort of fur coat. Hadn't his mother once wanted a fur coat? This would cheer her up. He trotted down the stairs and held it out to her.

"Look here, Mother. Look what I found in the bottom of Father's travelling bag!" Her eyes widened. Her hands trembled. Could it be? After all these years?

"My soul skin!" she cried. Her whole body was shaking now. He thought she was cold and so he offered to wrap the fur around her shoulders. She could hardly contain her joy. *Just like a woman*, he thought. *All they ever want is material things. Flowers, chocolates, jewellery, fur coats.* His wife was just the same.

"Well, I'll leave you to it, Mother. I must go upstairs and continue packing."

She sat there with her soul skin as it slowly melded back into the flesh of her body. It had been nearly forty years since she had been in her true form. Forty years since he had seen her dancing naked with her sisters on the beach in the moonlight. Forty years since he had stolen her seal skin to make her his bride. Forty years she had searched. Forty years he had hidden it in his travelling bag. Forty years away from her home, the sea. She tried to call out to her son, to say she must get to the sea immediately, but it was too late. She had transformed back into her seal shape and could not speak.

The son, who had packed everything away in the travelling bag that he wanted to take with him, jogged down the stairs in double time. *No point hanging around here*, he thought. A quick, obligatory cuddle with his mother and then he'd be off as he had a meeting at 4pm. He was rather surprised to see an enormous grey seal on the floor of the lounge.

His mother looked up at him with stormy eyes, but he did not recognise her. Where the deuce had it come from? He couldn't guess.

Where did seals live, anyway? By the sea? They were nowhere near the sea. Where was his mother? Had the brute eaten her? He knew nothing about the diet of seals, but it must have done because his mother was clearly gone. Suddenly, he had a brilliant idea. He pulled out the pistol that he had found in the back of his father's wardrobe and shot the filthy beast in the heart. *I'll get someone to taxidermy it*, he thought to himself. *It'll be the talk of the office!*

Rumple

You crawl into my bed
(Rumpled sheets,
The smell of yeast)
Just another man who believes
The lies my father tells:
That virgin cunny cures the pox.

You lie with me,
I lie to you.
(Rumpy-pumpy,
Sticky thighs)
A last hope for your withered prick
When mercury fails to do the trick.

I pull
The blanket made of wool
Over my head
To try and erase
Your face
Before the next one takes your place.

My virgin act begins anew.
You pay my father
Grease his palms
(a kind of alms)
To bed his one and only daughter.

To you this is nothing but a game,
And so you never even asked my name.

Author's note: *The myth of the virgin cleansing method dates back to the 16th century but gained prominence in 19th century Victorian England as a cure for sexually transmitted diseases such as syphilis or gonorrhoea. This myth persists today. According to Betty Makoni of the Girl Child Network in Zimbabwe, traditional healers advise HIV Positive men to have sex with young virgin girls as a cure for AIDS. UNICEF has attributed the rape of hundreds of girls to the virgin cleansing myth.*

Shattered Dreams

They were supposed to be made of white squirrel fur. When the witch woman cast the spell to adorn the filthy girl she clearly said "Vair," but the spirits have a will of their own. Perhaps they misheard. Perhaps they meant it to be a joke. All I know is they materialised as a pair of glass slippers. Verre.

The soot encrusted girl looked at them in horror. How was she meant to dance in shoes made of glass? The witch shrugged. "That's magic for you," she seemed to say.

Gingerly, she slipped them on her feet. Beads of blood appeared by her ankle like a line of miniature rubies. She sighed heavily. This was her chance to catch the Prince's eye. She hoped the pain would be worth it.

At the ball, the Prince's heavy boots chipped the heel of her left shoe. He did not seem to notice as her shoe filled up with blood. She continued to dance. What else could she do?

What happened next is up for debate.

The fairy tale will say that at the stroke of midnight she ran away, leaving behind one perfect shoe for the Prince to use to find her. The reality is less picturesque. She slipped in her own blood and fell down the stairs. The shoes shattered and cut her feet to ribbons.

Happily Never After

I was once married to a frog, only when I kissed him, he didn't turn into a prince.

Instead, I got warts.

A dozen times he took me dancing until the soles of my shoes wore out. On the thirteenth time he proposed. Lucky 13.

He had been married before. *She was an apple cheeked witch*, he said. *Cunning. Not like you, dear.*

At the time, I took it as a compliment. Perhaps I shouldn't have.

He brought me home to his castle (an Englishman's home is his castle), but there was a beast lurking in the shadows.

A rumpled creature with sullen eyes and three hairs growing from his pimply chin.

A teenager. A son.

I was the interloper. He let me know straightaway that I was not a patch on his sainted mother—a woman so perfect birds twittered around her head as she sang.

If she were here, the birds would shit on you (his eyes seemed to say).

His words pricked me like a spindle. I looked to my husband, his father to defend me. To say that I was not the evil stepmother in the story.

But he didn't.

Ribbit.

I baked gingerbread and other sweets to tempt the boy and buy his affection. After two weeks of marriage, I was asked to move out.

Not separated, he explained, *just separate. It's just that he doesn't want you in our house.*

But what do you want? I wanted to ask, but the words were a stale crust of bread in my mouth.

You must make allowances. The boy is grieving. He just lost his mother.

She's not lost. She's where you left her in Switzerland after the divorce.

Don't be such a heartless troll! He snapped. *We'll just find you a nice cottage somewhere nearby.*

Not too nearby, growled the boy.

The cottage was in a neighbouring village. It had been neglected for many years and ivy and roses swarmed over the bricks as if to suffocate it. I pricked my finger every time I opened the front door.

He visited me regularly at night to demand his conjugal rights as a husband. I slept through most of it.

This was the first five years of our marriage.

Why did I not wipe the pond slime from my lips and move on?

I loved him. (I guess.)

When the creature who despised me had grown a full beard, he flew from the nest and I moved back in.

Cuckoo.

It was bliss. We dined and drank rose-red wine and made love on the bear skin rug by the fire.

At Christmas, I plaited a dark red love knot into my long ebony hair, and he whispered into the shell of my ear, *Moonlit cruise.*

How romantic. Just the two of us? I asked.

He pulled back.

Sharpish.

No, just you. He doesn't want you here. It will spoil his Christmas.

My face was as pale as snow as he nibbled my neck. I bit my lip until it bled.

Why did you stay? Why did you stay when he delighted in such cruelty?

Because being second best is better than not being wanted at all.

It turned out to be a singles cruise.

Ribbit.

When I returned, I was surprised to see the boy had left me a gift.

It was a horse's head.

My husband merrily sang out, *Fa-La-La-La-Da!* and insisted I hang it up in my office to show the boy I liked it. (If your mother knew, it would break her heart.)

He's warming to you, he laughed.

I shivered.

So, it continued year after year until the Prince married and spent his holidays in another kingdom.

She was a common girl who expected to be treated like a princess.

A fool.

A ninny.

A goose.

But at least we were free.

On our twentieth Christmas, he would not look at me.

Did I know then?

How could I know?

It hit me like a curse.

I'm moving out.

Confused, I stumbled blindly through the dark of the forest.

You were always so cold, he said. *Frozen. You never once tried to be a mother to my son.*

Who is she? I rasped.

She is beautiful, pink and golden like a fruit. Young. When she speaks diamonds and rubies fall from her lips. Every word is a pearl.

I opened my mouth and a snake slithered out. Spiders slid down my face like tears.

My Frog King hopped away to another lily pad where he and his true love croak together.

I hope they choke.

So, I sit in this empty house and dream up punishments for them both. I would put her in a barrel studded with nails and then have her dragged behind a horse until she was dead, then drawn and quartered for good measure.

For him, I would prepare a pair of red hot iron boots and make him dance, like we danced all those years ago, until he fell down dead.

But it still won't bring him back.

CONTRIBUTORS

Another special thank you to the following people for their higher-level contributions to my Kickstarter campaign. This book exists because of your generosity.

Olivia Booy-falk
Cheryl & Nigel Habben
Luber Pinckard
Leila Pitchford
Carole & Rosie-Mai
Ashley Schoppe
Michelle Schoppe
Kristina Vincent
Carl Welday & Rebecca Tisdale Welday

ACKNOWLEDGEMENTS

Thank you first and foremost to my husband Thomas, the Amazing Spiderman. This is the best 50th birthday present I could have asked for. Hum-hum, tk tk tk, Olive Ewe and all that cliché rot.

Thanks also to my family, who have indulged my love of fairy tales and for buying me books through the years. Mum, are these creepy enough for you? GLT…wish you were here to see this. I hope you'd be proud.

To Ashley, thank you for championing my stories and encouraging me to submit a poem to your university literary magazine. They rejected it, but that was good because it belongs in here.

To David Hogue, modern day Atticus Finch and bow tie wearing curmudgeon. Thank you for your legal advice on terminology used in US court cases for *The Trial of Emily Scarlett*. My head was full of terminology from the UK Crown Prosecution Service and I did not want to rely on my fuzzy memory of episodes of Law and Order. Anything that is incorrect is down to me and not you.

Thank you to Kickstarter. Without a platform to raise money you would not be holding this book in your hand. Thank you to Stefan Keller for the beautiful cover illustration. The book would not look half as good without your creativity.

Most importantly a huge thank you to YOU. You who bought this book. You made this happen. When Thomas told me that he wanted to run a Kickstarter campaign to publish my book of feminist fairy tales, I nearly fainted from joy then nearly fainted again from terror. What if nobody bought it? But you did. You bought copies and extra copies to give away. You sent me encouraging notes. You bought it because you love me, and you bought it because you don't even know me. Thank you. With all my heart, I give thanks.

ABOUT THE AUTHOR

Heather Tisdale was born and raised in Louisiana. She has always had a flair for the dramatic and has been spinning tales from the moment she could speak. She graduated twice from Louisiana College, once with a degree that made her an interesting and well-rounded person and then went back to get her teaching qualification because being an interesting and well-rounded person does not get you a job. While in college she and her sidekick (who later became her husband) were exchange students for three months in London and became devoted Anglophiles. In 2004 they decided to live adventurously by leaving the American South and moving to the UK. She lived for a decade in England and now resides in a crooked pink house in rainy Wales with her husband Thomas and their rescued tarantulas and Giant African Land Snails. She is an author, an artist and an activist.

Lightning Source UK Ltd.
Milton Keynes UK
UKHW041456111019
351428UK00001B/32/P